WILD AMERICA
HABITATS

ARCTIC

By Melissa Cole

BLACKBIRCH®
PRESS

THOMSON
GALE

San Diego • Detroit • New York • San Francisco • Cleveland • New Haven, Conn. • Waterville, Maine • London • Munich

THOMSON

GALE

For more information, contact
The Gale Group, Inc.
27500 Drake Rd.
Farmington Hills, MI 48331-3535
Or you can visit our Internet site at http://www.gale.com

Photo Credits: Cover, all photos © Tom and Pat Leeson Wildlife Photography; pages 21, 23 illustrations by Chris Jouan Illustration

LIBRARY OF CONGRESS CATALOGING-IN-PUBLICATION DATA

Cole, Melissa S.
  Arctic / by Melissa S. Cole.
     v. cm. — (Wild America habitats)
  Includes bibliographical references (p. 24).
  Contents: What makes the Arctic unique? — Topography — Arctic plants — Arctic
  animals — Coping with cold — Humans and the Arctic.
   ISBN 1-56711-798-8 (hardback : alk. paper)
   1. Ecology—Arctic regions—Juvenile literature. [1. Arctic regions. 2. Ecology—Arctic
  regions.] I. Title. II. Series: Wild America habitats series.

  QH84.1 .C64 2003
  577.5'86'09113—dc21   2002153191

Printed in China
10 9 8 7 6 5 4 3 2 1

Contents

Introduction

The Arctic is located in the farthest regions of the north. It sits at the North Pole. It includes the ice-capped Arctic Ocean and the tree-less, marshy land called tundra. Of the many different habitats on earth, the Arctic is one of the most difficult places to survive. It is extremely cold, barren, and windy. Even so, many creatures are able to thrive in this harsh environment.

Marshy land called tundra is part of the Arctic landscape.

How Big Is the Arctic?

The Arctic is located at the North Pole. It extends throughout Alaska and northern Canada. Scandinavia and Russia also share this amazing habitat. The permanent ice that covers much of the Arctic Ocean extends over 2 million square miles (5.7 million sq km). In winter it expands to twice that size and encompasses an area even larger than Canada.

The Arctic doubles in size in winter.

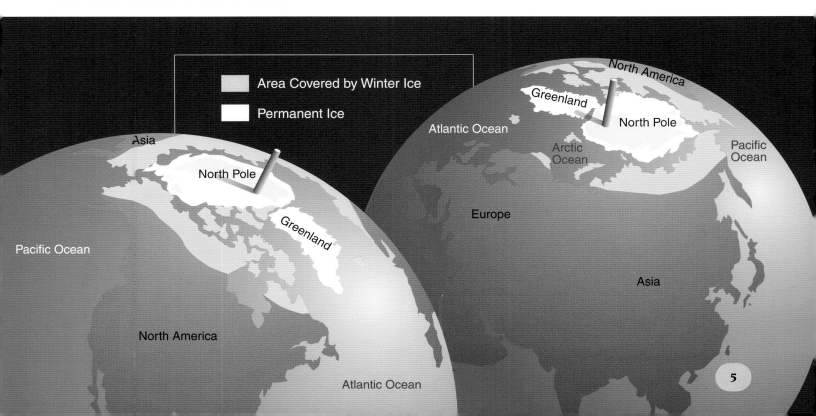

Area Covered by Winter Ice

Permanent Ice

What Makes the Arctic Unique?

The Arctic has an environment unlike any other on Earth. Its climate reaches extremes that are found nowhere else. Perhaps the most unique feature of the Arctic is aurora borealis—also known as northern lights. The sun causes this phenomenon. It sometimes sends out electrically charged particles that react with the earth's magnetic field. This combination results in shimmering streaks of yellow, pink, white, and green lights in the sky. Conditions for northern lights must be just right, though. The air must be cold and the sky clear, or one cannot see the brilliant lights.

The phenomenon known as northern lights may be seen in the Arctic on cold clear nights.

Climate

Air temperatures on the polar ice cap average 30°F (-1°C) but can drop below -58°F (-50°C) during dark winter months. The polar ice cap has hills and valleys made of ice. They have been carved out over time by wind. The Arctic Ocean can drop below freezing (32°F/0°C) without becoming solid ice because of the high concentration of salt in the water. A high concentration of salt in ocean water makes this water heavier than freshwater. The salt keeps ocean water from freezing or crystallizing as rapidly as freshwater.

Winter temperatures on the tundra range between 20°F and -70°F (-7° and -57°C). It can get colder when the wind picks up. Winds can be strong—from 30 to 60 miles per hour (48 to 97 km) per hour. Summer temperatures on the tundra rise up over 60°F (16°C), but can still dip below 30°F (-1°C).

Pieces of glaciers that break off and float in Arctic waters are called pack ice.

Topography

The northern ice cap is made up of gigantic floating ice islands called glaciers. Glaciers float on top of the Arctic Ocean and are up to 400 square miles (1,036 sq km) and more than 500 feet (152 m) thick. When glaciers melt, they float around the edges of the ice cap. These small chunks are called pack ice. Due to wind and water currents, the pack ice is constantly moving. This movement forms open areas of water called polynyas or leads.

Although precipitation only ranges between 4 and 20 inches (10 and 51 cm) per year, the tundra is a soggy place. Below the layer of tundra soil lies a permafrost layer. Permafrost is a permanently frozen layer of ground. It can be between 1,300 and 2,000 feet (396 and 610 m) deep. This spongy ground does not allow moisture to soak into it. Tundra can only support small, low-growing plants. It is scattered with ponds, lakes, and wetland areas. Taiga or boreal forest—a northern forest made up of evergreen trees as well as low growing birch and larch trees—surrounds the edges of the Arctic tundra. There is less wind here and temperatures are milder.

Boreal forests grow along the edges of the Arctic tundra. The climate there is milder than in other Arctic regions.

Caribou graze on grasses and mosses that grow on the tundra. **Inset:** Small dark hairs on some Arctic plants trap heat at the plant's surface.

Arctic Plants

The plants and animals that thrive in the Arctic have evolved ...que and fascinating ways to cope with their bleak surroundings. The Arctic tundra is a challenging place for plants to grow. All plants depend on the sun for energy, yet, for half of the year, the sun barely rises over the horizon. Arctic plants are forced to survive in cold temperatures that can freeze and damage them. Yet, despite these harsh conditions, many plants adapt to their environment and thrive on the tundra.

Even though tundra is covered by snow for much of winter, the roots and seeds of many plants survive below ground. In spring, mosses, grasses, and willows provide nutritious food for grazing animals, such as caribou and musk oxen. Summer transforms the tundra into a blaze of colors caused by masses of tiny wildflowers. During summer months, low-growing shrubs, such as huckleberries and wild blueberries, offer a tasty treat for many animals. Lichens (like-enz) are also common on the tundra. Lichens are made up of both algae and fungi. They look like crusty mosses. They coat rocks and bare ground.

Tundra plants can warm up quickly and stay warm even in cold conditions because many of them have leaves that are dark and hairy. Dark surfaces heat up quickly when the sun is shining because they absorb warmth. Fuzzy leaves trap heat against a plant's surface and protect it from the cold.

11

During dark winter months, the snow acts like a protective blanket for many plants. It blocks out chilling winds. In May, sunlight penetrates the snow and a few plants can start to grow. The Arctic growing season starts in June and only lasts 10 to 14 weeks. This is when the sun shines nearly 24 hours every day. Arctic plants must grow, flower, and set seed at a rapid pace to reproduce within this short growing season.

Arctic wildflowers only have 10 to 14 weeks to grow, flower, and reproduce.

Arctic Animals

There are several species of large animals that live in the Arctic Ocean. Seals and walruses glide through the water and feed on plentiful schools of fish. Many kinds of whales also inhabit this freezing ocean. Orca, beluga, and baleen whales are the most common. Baleen whales scoop up small fish with their gigantic mouths. Instead of having teeth, these whales have a special comblike substance called baleen. Baleen hangs from the tops of their mouths. It allows water to pour out while prey is trapped inside.

Harbor seals (top) and orca whales (bottom) live in the Arctic Ocean and feed on salmon and other fish.

Aside from whales, polar bears are the dominant predators of Arctic waters. They catch and eat seals that rest on the ice. Occasionally, they feed on baby beluga whales. When whales surface to breathe, polar bears may stun them with a blow from their huge paws and drag them ashore. Arctic foxes and ravens often follow polar bears across the ice to get a share of any leftovers.

The tundra is also home to large musk oxen and caribou. Other large grazing animals are also found on the tundra. Grizzly bears, moose, and elk are abundant in summer. They browse on willows and reeds that surround wetland ponds and lakes.

Large animals such as polar bears (top) and musk oxen (bottom) make their homes in the Arctic.

Dall sheep feed on grasses along the mountainous fringe of the tundra.

Ground birds such as ptarmigans (tar-mi-gans) and snow buntings also live on the tundra. They dig in the soil to find seeds and insects. Tundra swans, Canada geese, and old squaw ducks migrate to the tundra in spring and summer to build nests and to eat plentiful plants and insects.

Packs of Arctic wolves roam the tundra to find prey. Wolves are the major predators of this region. Wolf packs hunt both musk oxen and caribou. They follow herds and prey on animals that fall behind. Arctic foxes prey on voles, ground squirrels, and lemmings. They also eat leftovers from wolf kills.

Top: A ptarmigan eats seeds and insects.
Bottom: Arctic wolves roam the tundra in search of other animals to eat.

Coping with the Cold

Animals in the Arctic have adapted to their cold and snowy environment in a number of ways. Seals, whales, and walruses have thick layers of fat—called blubber—beneath their skin to keep them warm. Many animals—such as polar bears, musk oxen, caribou, and Arctic foxes—grow thick fur coats in the winter. They later shed them in spring and summer when it warms up.

Polar bears have hollow hairs, which provides excellent insulation. These hairs hold warm air close to their skin. They also help the bears to stay dry. Hollow hairs add buoyancy (ability to float) when these animals swim. Polar bears are not really white—they actually have black skin under their fur. Their hollow hairs are transparent, but they reflect the bright white of the tundra around them. A polar bear's dark skin absorbs heat from the sun and keeps bears warm in winter. They also have a thick fat layer below their skin that adds another layer of warmth.

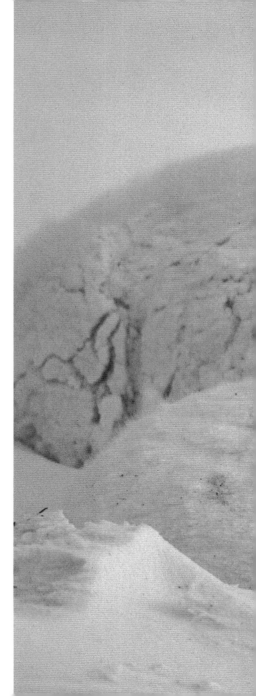

Polar bears snuggle together for warmth. These bears have hollow hairs that keep heat close to the skin.

Many Arctic animals have special feet for walking on top of deep snow without sinking. Large wide feet act like snowshoes. Arctic hares have huge, flat, furry feet that allow them to run quickly to escape predators. Ptarmigans can walk across the surface of snow with their feathered toes spread wide. Polar bears have enormous paws with tufts of hair growing between their toes. They have rough toe pads to keep them from slipping on the ice and stretchy, webbed skin in between each toe to help them swim.

Polar bears have giant paws that are wide and well suited for walking on top of snow.

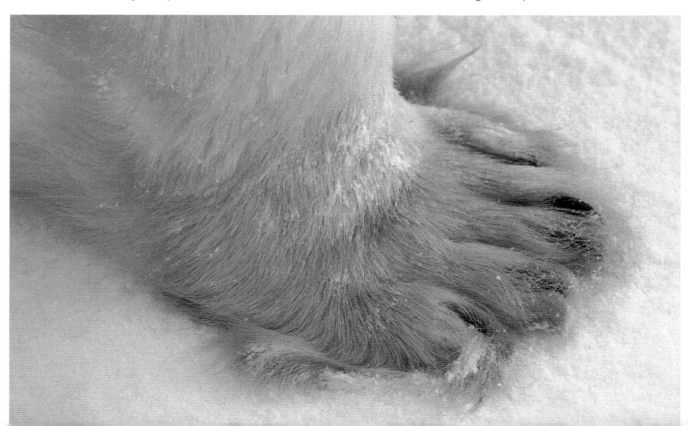

Ground squirrels, grizzly bears, and voles hibernate. Hibernation is like going to sleep for a long time. When an animal hibernates, its body temperature drops, its heartbeat slows down, and its breathing becomes barely detectable. It does not eat, drink, or produce waste. This conserves energy and protects the animal from extremely cold temperatures.

Some animals, such as nesting birds, caribou, and whales leave the Arctic during winter months to avoid the cold. In summer when the weather is warmer, these animals return to the Arctic to feed.

Animals that hibernate in winter, such as the ground squirrel, wake to feed when temperatures are warm and plants are in bloom.

Food and Water

Many species of Arctic animals have adapted to their habitat by having diets that change with the seasons. This allows them to survive extreme weather changes. They also get most of the water they need from their food. For example, grizzly bears dig up watery roots, eat dead animals, and hunt ground squirrels in springtime when snow still covers the ground. During summer, grizzlies feed on baby caribou and wild greens. In late summer, they stuff themselves with salmon and berries. When fall snow comes, bears eat roots and even seaweed before they dig a den to hibernate in during the harsh winter months.

Grizzly bears will hunt for food until they are ready to hibernate.

Food Chain

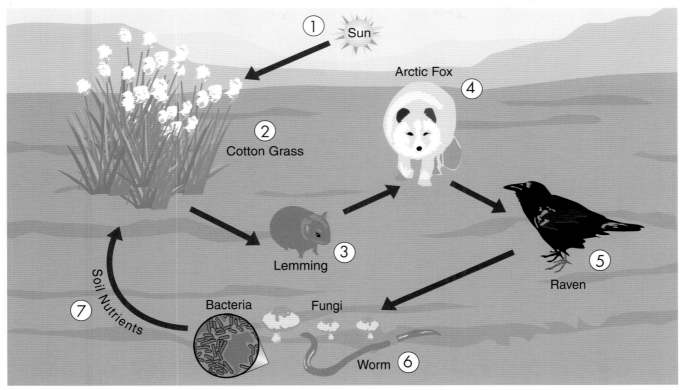

The food chain shows a step-by-step example of how energy in the arctic habitat is exchanged through food: The sun **(1)** is the first source of energy for all living things on earth. Green plants such as grasses and wildflowers **(2)** are able to use sunlight and carbon dioxide in the air to create sugar, which the plants use as food. The grasses are then eaten by the lemming **(3)**, which in turn becomes a meal for the arctic fox **(4)**. When the fox dies, the raven **(5)** will feed on its dead body. When the raven dies and falls to the ground, worms, fungi, bacteria **(6)**, and other decomposers feed on its body. Finally, these creatures or their waste products end up as soil nutrients **(7)**, which are then taken up by the roots of the grasses as part of their nourishment. The cycle then repeats.

Humans and the Arctic

Though few people live in the Arctic, there is a good deal of pollution. Air pollution forms a yellow cloud of smog. Drilling produces hazardous waste. It is stored in open pits on the tundra. This gives Arctic animals fewer places to live.

Many people are worried about global warming. Billions of molecules of gases in the atmosphere keep the earth warm. Today, the quantity of these gases has gone way up. If these gases increase too much, then the earth's temperature could rise. This would melt polar ice caps and raise the level of the ocean to dangerous heights.

One of the ways people can protect the Arctic is to set aside areas of land that cannot be developed.

People can also use alternative forms of energy regularly, such as wind and solar energy.

The Alaska pipeline carries oil from drilling sites to processing plants.

An Arctic Food Web

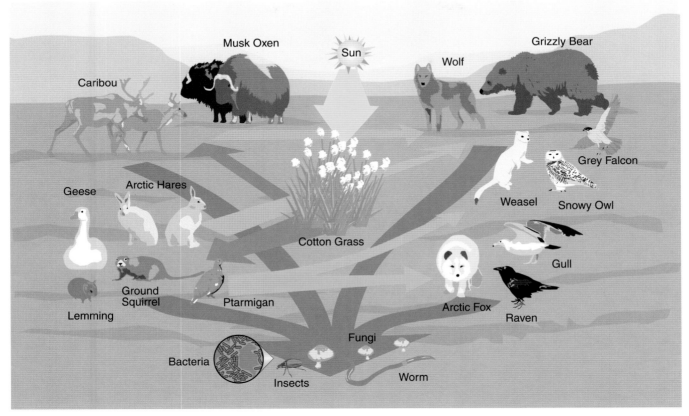

Food webs show how creatures in a habitat depend on one another to survive. The arrows in this drawing show the flow of energy from one creature to another. Yellow arrows: green plants which make food from air and sunlight; Green arrows: animals that eat the green plants; Orange arrows: predators; Red arrows: scavengers and decomposers. These reduce dead bodies to their basic chemicals, which return to the soil to be taken up by green plants, beginning the cycle all over again.

Glossary

Aurora borealis Also known as northern lights, this phenomenon is caused by the sun, which sometimes sends out electrically charged particles that react with the earth's magnetic field, resulting in shimmering streaks of yellow, pink, white, and green in the sky.

Decomposers Animals, such as earthworms, and plants, such as fungi, that eat dead tissue and return nutrients to the soil

Glacier A moving sheet or river of ice that slides from mountain regions toward the sea

Habitat The area in which a plant or animal naturally lives

Preserve A place where habitat is protected from development

Pack ice The moving chunks of ice that drift around the edge of the permanent icecap

Permafrost The layer of frozen soil beneath the tundra

Predators Animals such as wolves, that hunt other animals for their food

Scavengers Animals such as ravens that feed on animals that are already dead

Taiga The boreal or pine forest that surrounds the Arctic tundra

Tundra The marshy wetlands surrounding the Northern icecap

For Further Reading

Books

Brimner, Larry D. *Animals That Hibernate*. New York: Franklin Watts, 1991.
Kalman, Bobbie. *The Arctic World*. New York: Crabtree, 1988.
Paine, Stefani. *Arctic Whales*. San Francisco: A Sierra Club Book, 1997.
Sayre, April Pulley. *Tundra*. New York: Twenty-First Century Books, 1994.

Web sites

Arctic National Wildlife Refuge site
http://www.anwr.org/
Arctic Wildlife site
http://www.mnh.si.edu/arctic/html/wildlife.html

Index